IMAGES OF ENGLAND

FISH QUAY
NORTH SHIELDS

IMAGES OF ENGLAND

FISH QUAY
NORTH SHIELDS

PAT HOPE AND NORA TURNBULL

The
History
Press

First published in 2004 by Tempus Publishing

Reprinted in 2009 by
The History Press
The Mill, Brimscombe Port,
Stroud, Gloucestershire, GL5 2QG
www.thehistorypress.co.uk

British Library Cataloguing in Publication Data.
A catalogue record for this book is available from the British Library.

ISBN 978 0 7524 3379 0

Typesetting and origination by
Tempus Publishing.
Printed in Great Britain.

Contents

Acknowledgements

We would like to thank the following people for their kind permission:
Grace Nathan, Irene Turnbull, Joseph Rippeth, Joyce Bainbridge, Audrey McDonald,
Sylvia Stevens, Dave Marsh, Dorothy Robinson, Kathy Hall, Carol Brunton, Yvonne
Robson, Paula McVay, Ellen Heads, Selby Rix, Alan and Ina Thewlis, Susan Wright,
Jan Rutherford, Helen Nelson, Tilly Brunton, Joyce Grant, Denise Gracen, Steve
Conlan, Norma Anderson, Ray Kirk, Mrs Dickinson, Mrs Patterson and John
Livesley. Our thanks are also owed to Sharon Bailey – Isis Arts, Revd David C. Peel
– Cedarwood Trust, and Alaine Wright – Cedarwood Trust.

From the Royal National Mission to Deep Sea Fishermen Institute, we thank
Peter Dade, Paul Shone and Ann Alderson, and from the Local Studies department
of North Tyneside Library, we thank Eric Hollerton and Alan Hildrew.

Many thanks to Pat's husband Peter for standing by her and giving us good advice.

Bibliography

History resources:

The Origin of North Shields and its Growth – William S. Garson (1947)
Smith's Dock Journal – October 1930
Handbook to Tynemouth, and Co. (North Shields Schullermen)

Introduction

This book holds memories of the past in photographs from local people.

Besides the hardship of war, North Shields Fish Quay's past has had many happy memories until the decline of work there in the 1970s, but the folk have never given up hope. Fisher-folk are still fighting to keep their businesses afloat despite constant demolition and the building of luxury apartments around them.

For so many years, huge ships and cranes towering over the River Tyne were common views in the chimney-smoke-filled sky, and seen from homes and nearby factories. However, blue skies, luxury apartments and green retreats are today's focus.

The reader will find scenes of activities that are no longer with us, but are still part of our heritage. The images present a time when physical labour and the risk to life through sailing the waves in all weathers predominated in the area.

Ships gathered, filling the Fish Quay with their masts, fishing nets and lobster pots or, if the fleet had just arrived, with boxes of fish and the incomprehensible auctioneer. Men as well as women stood along the full length of the Fish Quay, all day and everyday and in all weathers, skinning and filleting fish for our dinner tables.

The information in this book was given to me in good faith but there is no guarantee of absolute accuracy. I hope readers have as much pleasure looking over the photographs as I have had in both collecting and selecting them.

Finally, to the friends who are no longer with us, I dedicate this book.

Pat Hope
August 2004

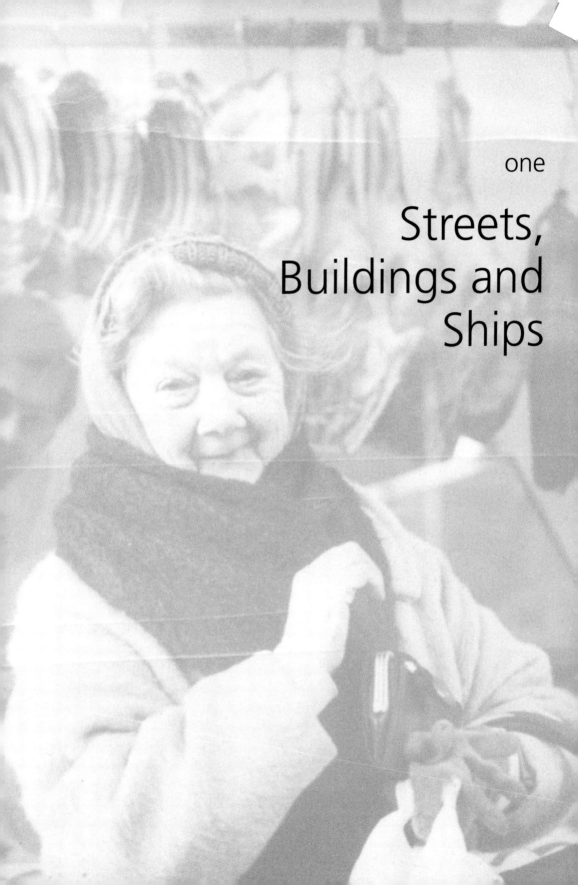

one

Streets, Buildings and Ships

North Shields' Fish Quay around the turn of the twentieth century. In the early 1870s, the Fish Quay was established by Tynemouth Corporation. They constructed a jetty close to the Low Lighthouse, and, soon afterwards, built a timber wharf along the length of Union Quay.

An aerial view of Smith's Dock in the 1940s. Smith's Dock opened in 1756 and built up over 200 years until the Smith family were one of the largest dry dock owners in the world. In around 1849, Smith's Dock purchased the Lime Kiln Shore, and another dry dock was made. It opened on 23 November 1852.

Right: An advertisement for Smith's Dock.

Below: Coble Dene, as it was before the construction of the Albert Edward dock. Behind the old tiled cottages on the left was a ballast hill. In this image, collier brigs are on the right and in front are stores of timber.

Robert Fredrick Wright sitting on the quay in the 1930s. He was the youngest of fifteen children; ten had died in infancy. He married Annie Fife Miller and had three children, Robert, Annie Fife and John.

Annie Miller and her cousin Ethel Leadbitter enjoy a walk along the Fish Quay in 1936.

Above left: Mrs Rosy Thewlis and her granddaughter Nan Smiles standing on Ropery Banks. Rosy lived in Stanley Street until a bomb from the Second World War killed her along with three children from the neighbourhood.

Above right: This advertisement to let shops and dwelling houses, dated July 1863, was posted in the North and South Shields *Gazette.*

Right: Robert Wright takes a break from his regular work of filleting fish while on board this fishing vessel at the Fish Quay.

Left: James Simmonds Rix, a hand rivetter, on board the trawler *Catherine* while undergoing repairs at Albert Edward Docks, around 1933.

Below: The Royal National Mission to Deep Sea Fishermen institute on the Fish Quay in 1956. The mission had been built in 1899 to house deep-sea fishermen. The mission also accommodated a hospital for the sick as there was none in the area at that time.

The Fish Quay gut around the 1960s. The Fish Quay saw a wealth of activity in its time; people from all over the world visited the area via road and sea. On the left, the fishermen's mission entertained the guests and fishermen once a year. It started with the Blessing of the Fleet, followed by a tribute to those who are lost at sea.

Looking over the Fish Quay from the bank side in the 1960s, the ice factory towers above the buildings. The tall white building was built around 1806–08 as the Low Light when the original one, built in the side of the walls of Clifford's Fort in 1727, was condemned.

This photograph was taken on the roof of the Haddock Shop on Union Quay looking across to the Sailor's Home. The Sailor's Home was built in October 1856 and opened by His Grace, Bishop Algernon the Good, who was also known as the sailor's duke. The handsome stone building that faces the quay was erected at a cost of £7,000 by the Duke of Northumberland. Out of this fund, £3,000 was subscribed by the public as an endowment fund. Sailors lodged there and had amenities suitable for a sailor's life. Looking over the buildings, cranes stand tall across the skyline.

Fishermen mending a net on the Fish Quay for their coming voyage on the sea in the 1930s.

Coxswain Raymond Oliver and his mates from Cullercoats Lifeboat Institute on one of their rescues on the River Tyne in the late 1960s. Raymond Oliver was a keen footballer in his earlier days.

Herbie Bridges, his wife Elsie and their friends at the Fish Quay in the 1930s.

In 1947 John Wright sits on his cousin John Cass's motorbike in the back lane of Addison Street.

The Haddock Shop yard, one of many yards that was busy along the River Tyne, around 1984. Today it has all disappeared and luxury apartments have been built on the site.

The Lifeboat House near the Fish Quay sands around the 1980s. It was built in the 1940s to house the lifeboats. The building has since been demolished.

Nellie Thewlis, (*née* Smiles), was born in 1902 and died in 1993. Behind her, in this 1960s photograph, Keith Harvey serves in the butcher's shop. Prices there have gone up a bit since then.

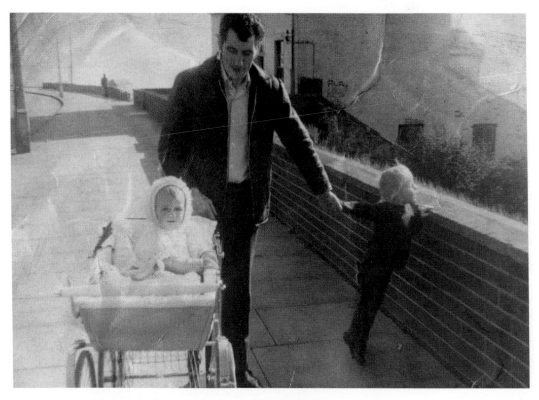

Jimmy Brunton taking his children, Nora, in the pram, and young Jimmy, curious to know what is over the wall, for a walk along Tyne Street in 1974. The High Light stands behind them.

The Camden Fisheries on Camden Street in 1974. Jimmy Brunton ran the business for about four years as a wet fish shop. Before then, it was a butcher's shop.

Fish Quay rocks and North Pier in 1978. Michael Hope and his sister Sylvia are around one of the rock pools. They lived at Dockwray Square.

Fish Quay beach with the DFDS Seaways ferry in the background. The ferry was on its way to Denmark in this 1978 photograph. It was one of many ferries that regularly left North Shields, sailing to Norway and Denmark.

Michael Hope, his brother David and his father Peter playing football in Dockwray Square in 1980. The High Light behind them was built around 1806–08 to serve as a beacon for ships coming to the Tyne.

The children, Paula and Tracy McVay enjoy a day out on the Fish Quay sands with Nora Brunton in July 1980.

Saville Street in 1969. F.W. Woolworth Ltd is one of the longest remaining stores in North Shields and the barrow, selling fruit and vegetables (seen to the side of the building), has been there for at least a lifetime.

On this 1981 evening, the sun sets, casting shadows over the Fish Quay sands. Note the two small boats tied up by the old jetty.

North Shields Fish Quay as it looks today. The prominent High and Low Lights and the old gas works tower in the skyline.

Looking up the River Tyne in the 1990s. Smith's Dock and offices dominated the bank side for over 200 years before being demolished to make way for buildings.

Above and below: The Tall Ships Race in 1993 dominated the Tyne from North Shields to Newcastle. The High Light stands in the background as do thousands of onlookers along both sides of the river.

Looking over the Fish Quay from Tyne Street, the Red Arrows show their aerobatic display over the North and South Pier during the Sunderland Air Show in 1993.

A view of Tynemouth Castle and Priory from the Tyne. The Castle and Priory are where monks set up the small fishing community that became North Shields in the thirteenth century. After Henry VIII came to the throne, he used the Priory spoils to fortify the Castle walls, and build the High and Low Lights, Clifford's Fort and the Spanish Battery.

In September 1980, the *Coriander* sailed the Indian Ocean. One of the crew members was James William Brunton from North Shields.

The SN34 *Bold Venture* stationed at North Shields Fish Quay in the 1980s. John Ord was the skipper.

The boat SN3 *Admiral* at Marconi Point in Cullercoats Bay was owned by Jeff Nugent in 1973.

The boat SN1 *Snow Flake* was owned by Jeff Nugent in 1988.

Jeff Nugent coming into Cullercoats Bay with his catch in June 1989.

USS *Rasing Eagle* on the River
Tyne in August 1968.

On the deep blue river, a tugboat called *Anglian* guides one of many ships to its destination up the Tyne.

Two ships, SN4 and LH100, sailing on the River Tyne the day of the Fish Quay Festival in the 1980s.

A North Shields ferry, the *Shieldsman*, transports commuters across the river to South Shields. The *Shieldsman* was retired from sailing in 1999 after ten or more years service.

The ship *Dea Skipper* out in the North Sea. Steven Brunton from North Shields was in the crew.

Wild weather storms against this oil-rig platform in the 1990s.

Thousands of cheering visitors lined the River Tyne to witness the stunning spectacle of the Parade of Sail in 1993. Prince Edward at the Tyne Bridge in Newcastle started the 8-mile procession of ships with their sails unfurled; it was the climax of Tall Ships Week on Tyneside. A record number of tall ships glided out to sea for the start of the race. Hundreds of private pleasure boats tagged along behind to form a colourful flotilla in the wake of the majestic ships. The ships were en route to Bergen in Norway before cruising to Larvik and racing again to Esbjerg in Denmark.

two
Work

A group of women working in one of the soup kitchens, probably Wellington Street in the late 1920s. Olive May Gardner, born 1904, is the third from the left in the back row. She lived with her parents in North Street, near Milbourne Place. Olive died in January 1986 in Waterville Road, at the age of eighty-one.

Arthur Dagg outside Collingwood Cottage in Tynemouth. Arthur was a member of the Tynemouth Volunteer Life Brigade in 1907.

Nicky Gracen (right) with his shipmates on the *Liberation of Denmark* in 1945.

In August 1916, Mr William Brunton received a reference from George R. Purdy & Sons. Mr Purdy built up his own fleet of steam-powered fishing boats and, in 1967, he sold his last boat to manage the Ranger factory ships.

Left: North Shields Fish Quay in 1918 with fishwife Cilla McDonald, who lived in Linskill Street at that time, on the right.

Right: At eighteen years, George Turnbull joined the Merchant Navy and was a stoker during the war. He was born in December 1921 and served on a number of ships.

A group of fishermen and fishwives on the fish quay in 1918. In the back row, second and third from the left are Cilla McDonald and Hannah Oliver.

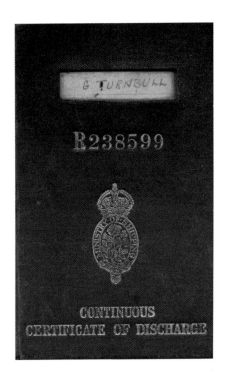

This page and top, following page: A record of the ships George Turnbull served on from 1946 to 1948 were recorded on his Continuous Certificate of Discharge.

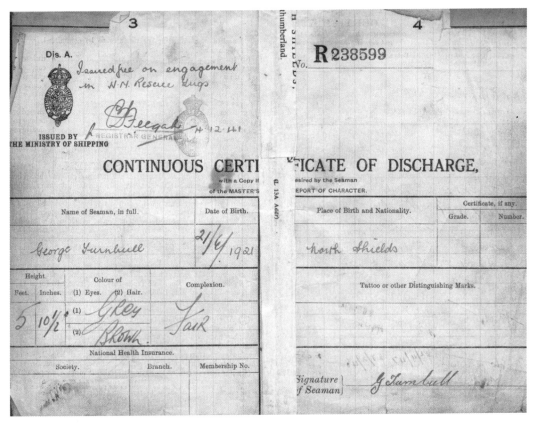

Above left: A fisherman, James McDonald, in 1929.

Above right: James McDonald on board ship with his shipmate from North Shields in 1929.

Finley McDonald, first on the left, aboard ship with his trawler-men shipmates in the 1930s.

Above left: On board a fishing vessel in 1934, Robert Wright stands between two of his shipmates.

Above right: Albert Brown (Ally) and Billy Binks on board ship in 1956. They put a bet on to see who could grow their hair longer than the other. Billy was known as North Shields' Elvis Prestley.

Eleanor and George Thewlis Gray and Cathy Woodhouse standing on the Albert Edward Dock in the 1940s. George died at the age of thirty-three in May 1948.

Ellis Fish Merchant's workers in 1970. From left to right in the back row are: Terry Christie, John Ellis, Tony Ishamor and Dave Smith. Front row: Alec Dale, Bob Foster, -?-, John Ellis snr, Bobby Robinson, -?-.

Jimmy Brown, a filleter, working for Harry Foskett's a wholesale fish merchant at Clifford's Fort in 1987.

Steven Brunton aboard the ship *Congena* in 1978.

From left to right: Tony Ishamor, -?-, and Bobby Robinson at a day's work, filleting fish at Ellis' in 1970.

In 1972, Bobby Robinson at his bench filleting fish at Ellis'.

Rupert Ellis preparing the net for the next day's fishing in 1987.

James Weatherstone, cleaning out the fish trays at the end of a working day on the Fish Quay in the 1970s. James died in 1993 at the age of ninety-two. By this time, he had witnessed many changes.

Jimmy Brunton, a barman on the RTA *Olwen* in August 1968. The ship was on its way to Scotland.

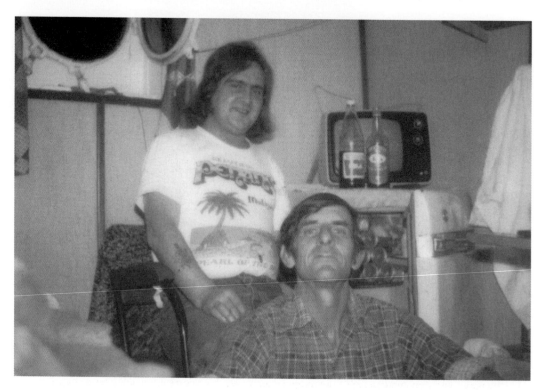

Jacky McVay (behind) and Jake Miller on board ship, relaxing after a hard day's work in the 1980s.

Barry Martin (Baz), Trevor Smith (Trev), and Steven Welsh (Tich) taking a well-earned rest after a day's fishing on the trawler *Crystal Sea* in 1983.

Johannes Syccama sorting out his catch of prawns off Eyemouth in 1984 with young Paul Turnbull(just seen, bottom right) watching. Johannes was born in Holland and lived in North Shields.

Judy Dobson, who lived in Knott Flats in 1985, watches over Willem Syccama's catch. Willem later became her husband.

Johannes Syccama (Yuppie) left and Jimmy Brunton wheeling their trays of prawns across Union Quay in 1985.

Bobby Robinson and Tony Ishamor fillet fish at Ellis' in 1970.

Joseph Bertram in the Royal Horse Artillery during the First World War.

Robert Wright was in the minesweepers during the Second World War.

Benjamin Miller (born in 1892), his wife Mary and their son. Benny served on HMS *Pembroke*.

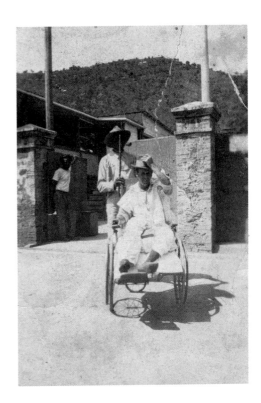

Joseph Rippeth (born in 1899) served in the Royal Navy in 1917. His parents, Thomas and Dora Rippeth (*née* Westall), lived in Charlotte Street at the time. The photograph was taken outside a hospital in South Africa, after Joseph suffered in an accident on his ship and damaged his kneecaps.

Jimmy Wilson at home on leave in Clive Street during the 1940s.

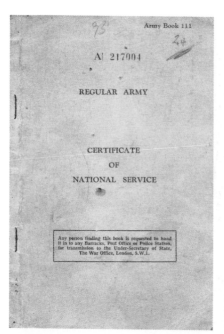

Left and below: This Certificate of National Service was issued to Selby Rix in September 1958 after two years in the army. He was enlisted in the Royal Artillery at Oswestry as a Regimental Signaller.

Page 1
Army
Book
111

SURNAME AND INITIALS _Rix S._

ARMY NO. _23585291_

GROUP NO. _58.18_

Discharge from Whole-time and Entry upon Part-time Military Service of a National Service Soldier

Designation of HQ, AER, or TA Unit to which the soldier is posted for part-time service :—

HQ AER/TA
c/o DEPOT RA
WOOLWICH S.E.18

CERTIFICATE OF DISCHARGE (To be retained by the soldier)   Page 2
Army
Book
111

Having completed whole-time service under the National Service Acts, 1948 to 1955, you are liable to further part-time service in the AER/TA unit to which you are posted until you have completed a total of five and a half years' service in all.

If this certificate is lost or mislaid no duplicate can be obtained.

Any unauthorized alterations of the particulars in this certificate may render the holder liable to prosecution under the Seamen's and Soldiers' False Characters Act, 1906.

| ARMY NO. _23585291_ | RANK _Gnr L/Bdr_ |

SURNAME (Block Capitals) _Rix_

CHRISTIAN OR FORE NAME(S) (Block Capitals) _SELBY ADAMSON_

UNIT, REGT. OR CORPS for which enlisted _ROYAL ARTILLERY_

from which discharged _ROYAL ARTILLERY_

Service began on _18.9.58_ at _OSWESTRY_

Effective date of discharge from whole-time service _17 SEPTEMBER 60_

Total amount of full-time reckonable service _2 YEARS_

Reason for discharge _NS RELEASE_

Description of Soldier on Completion of Whole-time Service

Date of birth _18.7.37_   Height _5_ ft. _4½_ ins.

Complexion _PALE_   Eyes _GREEN_   Hair _BROWN_

Marks and Scars (visible) _SIDE L/KNEE & L/SHOULDER SCAR_

Trade Qualifications

CIVILIAN TRADE _SHIPWRIGHT._

SERVICE TRADE _REGTL SIGNALLER._

FINAL EMPLOYMENT _REGTL SIGNALLER_

Courses and Tests passed _3 STAR SIGS COURSE_

Swan Hunter's Mould Loft, in 1964. From left to right: Selby Rix, Arthur Stevenson, -?-, Dave Nancarrow, Dave Stonebanks and Tom Lockhart play dominos on their break in the canteen.

Smith's Dock in April 1973, outside Mould Loft. From left to right, in the back row are: John Blackburn, Ted Gould, John White and Alan McKever. Front row: Tom Kennedy, Brian Baistow and Selby Rix. In front of the men is Stan Hudson.

On board the *British Adventure* in 1961, from left to right are: Geordie Sunderland, Adam Smith, Brian James, -?-, -?-, -?-, Chow Norman and Stewy Oat. The group relax around a table with their pints. The two men standing are Tom Wright and Jake Miller.

In 1962 Tom Wright and Geordie Heads from the Royal Fleet Auxiliary sailed on board the ship *Tide Surge* to the Seychelles.

Taking a break from work on the Fish Quay in the 1970s, Rosie Brunton sits in the middle of these women.

William Brunton sailed on the *British Yeoman* that was torpedoed in 1942.

12581

B. & D. 30.

GENERAL REGISTER AND RECORD OFFICE
OF SHIPPING AND SEAMEN,
Llantrisant Road, WOOD STREET SCHOOLS,
Llandaff,
CARDIFF.

CERTIFIED EXTRACT FROM THE LIST OF THE CREW

of the "BRITISH YEOMAN" Official Number 147491 transmitted by the

Owners – British Tanker Co. Ltd.,

to the Registrar-General of Shipping and Seamen under the provisions of Section 255(2), of the Merchant Shipping Act, 1894.

Name	Age	Nationality (stating birthplace—if British)	In what capacity engaged	Particulars of termination of Service		
				Date	Place	Cause
William Edward Brunton	22	No.S.	Sailor	Supposed drowned	vessel	torpedoed & sunk 14/7/42.

I CERTIFY the above to be a true Extract from the list of the crew referred to. The ship is stated to have been

Examined by

Assistant Registrar-General of Shipping and Seamen.

Fee Two shillings and sixpence   Dated this 27th day of November 1942.
(including fee for search)

A certificate served to the parents of William Brunton, who lost his life when his ship was struck by a torpedo. The ship sank in July 1942 when William was only twenty-two years old.

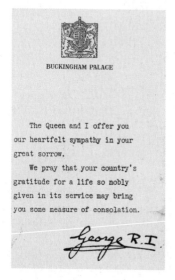

BUCKINGHAM PALACE

The Queen and I offer you
our heartfelt sympathy in your
great sorrow.
    We pray that your country's
gratitude for a life so nobly
given in its service may bring
you some measure of consolation.

George R.I

Left: A copy of a telegram sent to Mr and Mrs Brunton concerning the death of William.

Right: George Turnbull from 6 Appleby Street served in the Royal Navy during the Second World War. This image was taken in around 1939.

three

Events and
Pastimes

The Blessing of the Fleet, performed by the Royal National Mission to Deep Sea Fishermen Institute. The mission was opened in 1899 and this is one of their early blessings, which were held every year. In 1978, the service became a big event at the end of May, lasting a whole weekend. It became known as the Fish Quay Festival.

CHOLERA.

Every House in the Village must be immediately White Washed, Outside and Inside.

Hot Lime will be provided, free of charge.

Every Nuisance to be at once removed.

The Houses to be freely Ventilated, and Good Fires maintained.

Chloride of Lime to be had, free of charge, at the Colliery Store House.

Medicine to be obtained on the First Symptom of Bowel Complaint, and on no account to be deferred.

A notice about cholera and how to deal with it in the early days.

Mr and Mrs Arthur Dagg and family taking a walk along the North Pier in 1908. They lived at Collingwood Cottage and Arthur was a chemist. The original North Pier was completed in 1895 and showed signs of being unsound. In 1897 110ft of the pier collapsed and it was decided to reconstruct the pier in a straight line, taking advantage of the shale bed that gave the foundations more support. The contract was given to the firm of Sir John Jackson, rebuilding commenced in 1898 and was completed in 1908.

Left: James, Arthur and George Turnbull at the Milbourne Carnival, *c.* 1928. They live in North Street or Appleby Street with their parents.

Right: Audrey McDonald, in her fancy frock and bonnet, came second in a competition at the East-End Carnival in September 1937.

Herbie and Elsie Bridges enjoying themselves on Tynemouth Long Sands in the 1930s. The outdoor swimming pool is in the background.

GRAND ORDER
OF
WATER RATS
HOUSE
DINNER

SAVOY
HOTEL
LONDON
SEPT. 21st 1947

GUESTS
OF
HONOUR

STAN
LAUREL·

OLIVER
HARDY

Menu from the 'Water Rats - House Dinner',
held in honour of Laurel and Hardy.
(Artwork by Louis Valentine.)
(By courtesy of Peggy Valentine.)

An advertisement about Stan Laurel and Oliver Hardy in 1947. Stan Laurel once lived in North Shields.

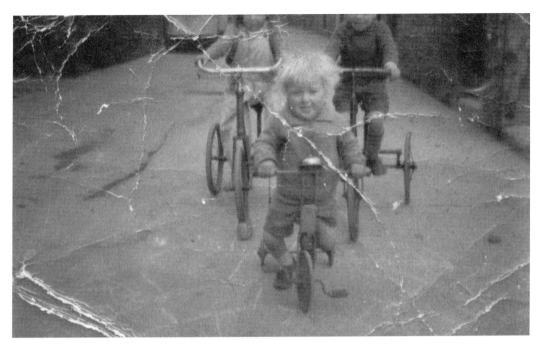

Eileen Duncan with John and Robert Wright in the back lane of Addison Street in 1949. Eileen's grandma was John and Robert's aunt on their mother's side.

Ann Thewlis and her uncle Jacky Thewlis on the sea front at Tynemouth in 1950.

The boating lake and Tynemouth Plaza in 1953. Joseph Rippeth, who was a carpenter by trade, made this sailing boat for his son Joseph. The Plaza delighted thousands of people over the years until early one Saturday morning on 10 February 1996 a fire broke out, causing extensive damage to the building. It was consequently demolished.

Kathy Boylen's confirmation at St Cuthbert's RC church in Bedford Street in 1953. She lived with her parents, merchant seaman William Boylen and Isabella at Stephenson Street.

Patricia Nathan and her sister Linda standing at Collingwood's Monument in 1963. The original cannons were on the HMS *Royal Sovereign*. Vice-Admiral Cuthbert (later Lord) Collingwood was born in September 1748 in Newcastle. He joined the Navy in 1761 at the age of twelve, and first sailed on the HMS *Shannon*. He married Sarah, the daughter of John Erasmus Blackett' the Mayor of Newcastle, in June 1791. He sailed with Lord Nelson on the *Royal Sovereign* during the Battle of Trafalgar in October 1805. Collingwood died on the morning of 7 March 1810, aged sixty-one.

A group of boys camping in Hexham in 1962. From left to right, the boys are: Charlie Manning, Joe Wanless, Terry Walsh and Sid Buglass.

Steven Brunton and his cousin George paddling on Tynemouth Long Sands in 1969. They lived in Gardner Street.

Linda and Patricia Nathan at Collingwood's Monument in around 1962. The Lifeboat Museum, Collingwood Cottage and Spanish Battery stand behind the monument.

Ken O'Neil, Hank Hardy and Terry Walsh on Tynemouth Long Sands in the early 1970s. The Grand Hotel stands stately above them.

On 12 December 1971 a Christmas party was held for the orphan children. The Royal National Mission to Deep Sea Fishermen institute's Ladies Committee arranged a party every year for these children.

Tynemouth in 1972. June Guens is seen here with her son Danny, Tom Wright and his daughter Dawn. June and Danny were on holiday from Belgium. Tynemouth pool was closed in 1990, and in 1996 the pool was turned into a rock pool.

Saville Street, North Shields on one evening during the 1960s. In this photograph, Mickey Anderson, Margaret Harvey, Jackie McVay and Terry King stand on the corner of the street. Saville Street is the main thoroughfare into town with businesses and shops on both sides of the street.

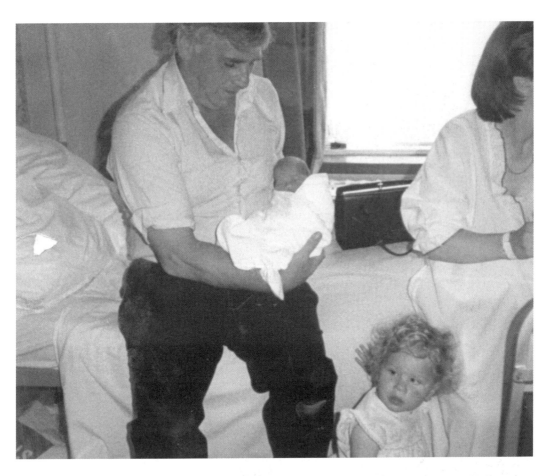

Above: Renwick Smith holds his recently born granddaughter Angela Toby in 1984. Also in the image are his daughter Carol and his granddaughter Michelle Toby. They lived at The Nook at that time.

Right: Mavis Smith on holiday at the Sunnyside Guest House in Keswick in 1969. The proprietor of the guesthouse gives Mavis a firm hold. Mavis lived at The Nook with her husband Renwick.

Left: Steve Drury's fishing tackle shop on Saville Street in 1996. From left to right, in the front row are: Ashleigh Dumbell, Paul Turnbull, Andrew King, Dave Marsh, Carl Redpath, Mark McDonald and Dean Redpath. Micky Tait stands at the back on the right.

Below: A group of ladies on a day trip to Scarborough in 1991. Mrs Nora Turnbull on left, Mrs Crombie in front and Irene Turnbull in a stripped dress.

Christopher Robson standing on a turtle that had been dragged on shore when caught up in a fishing net in 1990. His neighbour Jimmy Brown holds him.

The Fish Quay Festival, held across Union Quay and the Dolphin Quay in 1992, entertained thousands of canny people who came to North Shields. Joanne Turnbull from King Edward's School was one of many children who took part in a pageant.

Paula McVay and Nora Turnbull with their children. Paul Turnbull and the McVay children, John, Amy and Katie, watch the bands perform on stage at the Fish Quay Festival in 1998.

A group of boys at the Fish Quay Festival in 1998. Musicians from countries worldwide came to the Fish Quay for a weekend at the end of May. From left to right are: Paul Turnbull, Shaun Thompson, Robert Farman, Dean Redpath and Andrew King.

Michael Hope on *The Nemo*, a wreck finder, outside the River Tyne in 1987. Michael has a 25lb cod in his arms.

Angela Toby and Kerry Willis at the Sea Cadets in Tynemouth in 1998.

Nicky Gracen served in the Merchant Navy as Swamper Gracen in his younger days, and pays his respect at the Cenotaph in Tynemouth in this photograph, taken in 1989.

From left to right are: Valerie and James Eastern, Dennis Ridsdale (at the back), June Luke, Terry Walsh, Eric Luke, Irene Turnbull and Mr and Mrs Jimmy Slessor. The group are on a day trip to Blackpool from North Shields in 1979.

Muriel and David Burke at Knott Flats in the 1980s. David worked as a butcher on Church Way for many years.

Margaret Thompson, Muriel Burke and their friend Linda after a game of bingo at King Street's social club in the 1980s.

Arthur and Lilian Kennywell enjoying a Christmas party at King Street's social club in the 1980s.

Willem and his brother Johannes Siccama at Eyemouth are being watched over by Jimmy Brunton and Paul Turnbull in 1984.

Judy Dobson and Nora Turnbull on the fishing boat *Sean Too*, going to Eyemouth in July 1985 to see the Herring Queen contest.

On a trip out to sea, Paul Turnbull caught a whopper for his dinner. He is seen here with Robert Farman, in around 1997-98.

In 1954 Robert and Jean Jefferson were married. Jean worked at a scrap-yard and later at Haggies rope factory. Robert, her husband, worked in the shipyard.

Larry Forster marrying Mary Ellen Thewlis in 1956.

Left: Alan Thewlis marrying his lovely bride Ina at Holy Trinity church in 1956.

Below: Joyce Bainbridge, George McDonald, Nana McDonald and James McDonald after the marriage of Gillian McDonald and Robert Burn at the registry office in Norfolk Street in 1979.

On the wedding day of Carol Smith and Phillip Toby on 1980, a group pose outside the registry office on Norfolk Street with their guests Hannah Toby, Harriet Cook, Meg Thompson and Mavis Smith.

Rosie McNeil and her husband Donald at Simon and Ruth Gilcrist's wedding reception at the Garrick's Head in 1989. Ruth, Jimmy and Maureen Wilson are in the background.

James Davy and Dorothy Watts outside St Peter's church in the Balkwell in 1968. James was in the third Regiment of the Paras.

The 1987 marriage of George and Lesley Turnbull with their parents on either side. The parents of the groom are George and Nora Turnbull, while David and Muriel Burke stand with their daughter.

Mr and Mrs Danny and Christine Brown outside the registry office in Northumberland Square in the 1950s.

John Wright and Ann Watts outside St Peter's church on their wedding day in July 1967. From left to right, the guests here are: John Harrison with his baby John, Jack Sheldon, Walter Cass, Dora Watts, Sally Watts, Margaret Sheldon, George Watts, Elizabeth Cass, Dianne Cass, Steven Cass, Robert Wright, Anne Harrison, Freddy Watts, Annie Wright, groom John Wright, Robert Wright, the bride Ann Wright, Thelma Wright, Mary Bruce, Doris Watts, Irene Greyburn, Jack Greyburn, Jackie Watts, Tom Hendrickson, Norman Crosby, Michael Watts and John Cass.

four

Pubs

Nellie Thewlis (*née* Smiles) and Meg Carr in The New Clarendon on Appleby Street in 1939. The old Clarendon was demolished in 1901 to make way for the extension of Smith's Dock. It closed in 1997 after its owner Keith McAlister fought to keep the business afloat. He spent hundreds of pounds to keep burglary and vandalism at bay, as no insurance company would take the risk.

Dave Artley and his wife Tina, Ann Watts and John Wright on a night out at 'The Jungle' (The Northumberland Arms) in the 1960s.

The Jungle was part of the Northumberland Arms on the New Quay. Lilian Burns was proprietor of the pub and her Aunt Lil, next to her, was the barmaid in 1982.

Merlin Jackson, Joan Main, Denise Malvern and Gitas at The Jungle in 1984.

Alan Jackson, Betty Dunning, Jerry ? and Andy Mills at Yhe Jungle in 1984.

Harry Vandeeny and Terry Walsh at the Cresta Club in 1965.

Terry Walsh and Irene Turnbull at the Colin Campbell on Camden Street in 1969. The club has since been demolished.

A night out with a friend. Shirley Brown and Irene Turnbull at the Cresta Club in 1969.

Bob Foster, Rosie Carr, Bobby and Dorothy Robinson at the Cresta Club in 1970.

Bobby and Dorothy Robinson, Bob Willis and Eddie Wood at the Cresta Club on Camden Street in May 1971.

Meg Meek, Irene Turnbull and Ella Smith enjoy an evening of entertainment at the Cresta Club on Camden Street in 1971.

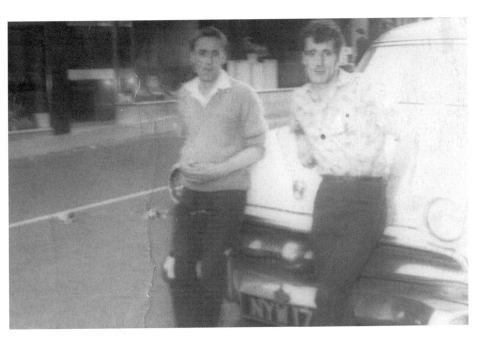

Outside Uncle Tom's Cabin in Bedford Street in 1960 are George Wilson and Jimmy Brunton. They both worked for Central Taxis at the time. In the early 1970s, Bedford Street and the surrounding area underwent a major regeneration; a new shopping forum, the Beacon Centre, was built, and a new library was added to Northumberland Square in 1974.

A group of young men enjoy a night out at the Park Hotel in Tynemouth in 1965. In the photograph are Terry Walsh, Ed Barbrook, Albert Cheshire, Ken Smith and Ally Smith.

Ann Robinson, Meg Meek, Irene Turnbull and Jackie Sturrock at Uncle Tom's Cabin in 1967– all friends together.

Flea Hunter, Martin Bailey, Ally Smith and Terry Walsh at Uncle Tom's Cabin in 1968.

Ann and June Jeffries, Irene Spears, Christine Jeffries and Liz Henderson on a night out with friends at Uncle Tom's Cabin in 1969.

Micky Anderson, Jacky McVay, Don Frazer and Bob Watson at Uncle Tom's Cabin in Bedford Street in 1969.

Jackie McVay, Terry King, Gill Harvey, Ray Wiseman and Bob Watson at Uncle Tom's Cabin in 1969. These young men were all seamen who sailed with the Royal Fleet Auxiliary.

Bobby and Dorothy Robinson at Uncle Tom's Cabin in 1972.

Freddie Leck, Bobby Robinson, Stan Carr and Dorothy Stanners at the Alnwick Castle in 1968.

A night out at the Alnwick Castle in 1968. In this photograph are Terry Walsh, a trained French polisher, Bill Thompson, the manager of the Alnwick Castle on Saville Street, and Alan Burns, manager of The Jungle.

Billy Robinson, Dot Patterson, Bobby Robinson and Eddie Wood at the Alnwick Castle in 1971.

All friends together in the 1980s from left to right: Debbie Newby, Carol Toby, Jacky Hewitson and Angela Jackson.

Fish Quay locals enjoying a night out in Whitley Bay in the 1960s. In the photograph are from left to right: John Wright, Ann Watts, Tina Artley and her husband Dave.

The Robinson family, Philip, Eva, Bobby, Dot and auld Billy Robinson at the Colin Campbell on Saville Street in 1971.

Freddie Leck, John Carr (Maxi) and Bobby Robinson having a drink in 1968.

Bobby Robinson, John Carr (Maxi) and Freddie Leck at the Gardner's Arms in 1968.

At the Gardner's Arms on Gardner Street in 1969, from left to right are: -?-, Dot Harvey, Jacky McVay, Gill Harvey, Margaret Harvey, -?-, and Terry King (front).

John and his brother Jimmy Gray, both welders in the docks, sitting on the right at the Bewicke in Howdon in the 1960s. Jimmy's son Jim raced greyhounds at Brough Park for years.

The Jolly Girls at the Ballarat on Saville Street in the 1980s. Only a few names are known: Dolly Walker, Margaret Connelly, Helen White, Elsie Walker, Liza Leck, Jinny Longstaff, Audrey Davison and Betty Piers are amoung those in this photograph.

Happy days in the 1980s. Some pictured here are: Kennedy Burgo, Robert Herman, Bobsa, Scampi, Dean, Dowser, Jake and Justin Santos.

Alex Lattimer, Maureen McGinty and Nora Turnbull enjoy a drink and good company at the Stanley Arms in 1982.

Dorothy Denley, Paula McVay and Denise Gracen enjoy an evening away from home at the Terminus Social Club nicknamed the Busman's on West Percy Street in 2002.

Karen ?, Gwen Peters, Angela Jackson, Yvonne Smith, Mrs Mavis Smith, Jackie Hewitson, Catherine Hedley and Mavis Lively at the Albion (Top House) on Nile Street.

five

People

Annie Fife Miller poses for the camera at Elliot Studio on Bedford Street in the 1930s.

Evelyn Brunton, the daughter of William and Margaret Brunton from Algernon Terrace, poses for the camera at Elliot Studio in the 1920s.

Margaret Turnbull with her son Arthur in North Street in 1911.

Arthur Turnbull posing for the camera at Elliot Studio in 1912. An address written on the back of the photograph for enlargements is as follows: Mrs Westwater, 3 Ropery Banks, North Shields.

James and Arthur Turnbull, who lived with their parents in North Street, at Elliot Studios in Bedford Street in 1915.

In 1927, James Henry Thewlis with his children, Robert, John and Mary Ellen, outside their home in Milbourne Place or South Street.

Margaret Miller (*née* Bertram) (in the middle), with her friends Tom and Nelly from London in the back yard at Addison Street. Her friend Tom looks very much like the comedian Norman Wisdom!

Rosie Ann Thewlis (*née* Watson) poses for the camera at Elliot Studios in September 1929.

Robert Wright is dressed in his Sunday best for the camera in around 1930–31. He was a trawlerman for most of his life.

Around the 1950s, Arthur (left) and George Turnbull (right), labourers at Smith's Dock, lived on Howdon Road, and Jimmy, who worked at the Haddock Shop on Low Street, lived at Cedarwood Avenue.

Tommy Gardner from Sibthorpe Street poses for the camera at Saville Studios on Saville Street in April 1937.

In July 1935, James Henry Thewlis poses with his granddaughter Mena Smiles. She is described as having blue eyes and a fresh complexion.

Margaret Evelyn Lloyd (*née* Brunton) lived at Algernon Terrace in 1939. She sadly died from Leukaemia at the age of twenty-six.

Etty, the daughter of George and Grace Clark, was eighteen years old in this photograph, which was taken in 1939. She was born in Middle Street or Milbourne Place where her parents lived. She worked at Haggies rope factory and later was a barmaid at the Stanley Arms.

Nora Turnbull (*née* Gray) mother of Nora and Irene was born in 1926 at the Bullring. She worked at the pickling factory and lived on Howdon Road.

In 1942 Margaret Evelyn Lloyd stands at the door of 13 Algernon Terrace with her only son James.

Annie Wright and her brother John, her cousin John Sheldon and her half cousin Robert Duncan in the back lane of Addison Street in 1947.

Eileen Duncan and Robert Wright in back lane of Addison Street in around 1947.

At the Fish Quay in 1948, Nora Gray, Ida Wilson, Ella Hutchinson and Arthur Turnbull pose for the camera.

Isabella Boylen, who lived at Ropery Stairs, the Bankside on the Fish Quay, in around 1921.

Arthur, the son of Arthur and Ida Turnbull, in 1939. Look at the frown on his face!

In the back land of Addison Street 1949, John Wright holds a puppy.

John Wright and Eileen Duncan in the back lane of Addison Street in 1949.

Robert Wright and his brother John in Addison Street in 1949. Do you remember the game Hopscotch? A piece of chalk and a stone are all that's needed to play the game.

Robert Wright and Eileen Duncan in the back lane of Addison Street in 1949 holding a dog each. You don't see many of those child's bikes around nowadays!

Nora, George, Ella and Arthur Turnbull at the Fish Quay in July 1948. The boy in front of them is Arthur, son of Arthur and Ida.

Henrietta and baby Carol Stewart from Milburn Place in the late 1940s.

Robert Wright, Henrietta Duncan, Annie Wright and Adam Duncan enjoying a sunny afternoon at the Fish Quay, in the late 1950s.

Nora and her sister Irene Turnbull, aged five and three years old respectively. The sisters lived on Howdon Road with their parents, Nora and George Turnbull. This photograph was taken at Saville Studios in 1952.

In the yard at 53 Brunton Street in 1952 the Robinson children, Billy, Brian, Bobby and Ann, pose for the camera. They were the children of William and Mary Robinson.

Tom Wright and Victor Wales in the back lane of Addison Street in 1956.

Annie Fife Wright and Ann Wright with Duke and Prince, the dogs, in the backyard at 25 Gardner Street in the late 1960s. The flat was one of a few that belonged to the Scandinavian Lutheran church. It was built at the top of Borough Road in 1868 from ballast stone brought from Norway. The Norwegian sailors stayed there at some time and a rubber company bought the flats from them, renting them out. The church was closed in October 1966 and was later demolished.

William and Margaret Brunton at Stanley Street West in 1960. William was an assistant Quay Master and fought in the Second World War. He died in 1969.

Kathy, Isabella (*née* Urwin) and Jean Boylen lived at Stephenson Street in 1949.

Outside William Hoggs & Co., on Lawson Street in 1956 are: –?–, Tom Foster, Joan Ferguson, May McCulloch, Tom Wright and John Foggett.

Jimmy Brunton, his son Steven, and the German shepherd dog Andy in the backyard of Gardner Street in 1967. This house and backyard once belonged to the manager of Uncle Tom's Cabin, Lily Flart.

In September 1969, Nora Brunton stands at her home in Gardner Street with her stepsons, Steven, David and Michael Brunton. Anne Lloyd stands behind Nora.

Helen Wilson, baby James, David and Ruth in the backyard of their home Howdon Road in 1970.

John, Norma and Alan Anderson on one side of Coach Lane off the back lane of Stanley Street West, backing on to Alexander Scott Park, in the 1960s.

George Turnbull, Steven Brunton and Leslie Philips in the backyard of 6 Howdon Road in 1971.

Annie Fife Wright with her daughter Ann Harrison and her daughters-in-law, Thelma and Ann Wright in Linskill Terrace at Christmas 1973.

Tom Foster, Peter Hope and Walter Watson standing outside their homes on Tyne Street and Dockway Square in 1979. These two-storey maisonettes were vacated in 1980 for demolition.

A family get together around 1979–80. From left to right are: Ronnie Stonebanks, Muriel Burke, Joe Goicoechea in the front, and David Burke and Nancy Brown behind.

Tyne Street in 1979. These children were celebrating Lisa Watson's third birthday. Included in this image are: Joanne ?, David Hope and his sister Sylvia, Leslie Watson and her daughter Lisa, Samantha Richardson, Linda ?, Michael Hope and Paula Richardson, on the far right.

John William Miller (front row, first left) from 20 Addison Street with his fellow Dockers. John was born on 18 January 1870 at the Spanish Battery in Tynemouth. His parents were Benjamin Jerome Miller and Selina Agnes (née Conaty). John married Margaret Bertram and worked as a dock labourer. They had fifteen children, five of whom died in infancy.

The Trotter boys in the 1920s: from left to right: Billy, Selby, Edgar, George and Joseph.

The Trotter girls in the 1920s from left to right: Alice Pooley, Kitty Hamilton, Meg Taws, Sarah Anne Rix, Mary Baverstock and Lily Church.

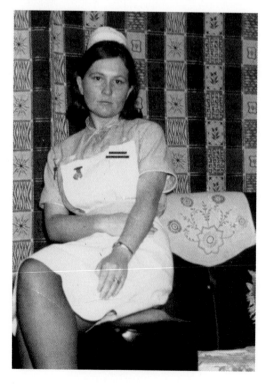

Early in the 1960s, at the age of seventeen, Dorothy Watts trained to be a nurse at Preston Hospital and Tynemouth Jubilee Infirmary. She stayed at Preston Towers for a short time.

Eddie Wood, Bobby Robinson and his father Billy at the General Havelock in 1970 on Saville Street.

Mrs Peggy Hall sitting on a wooden horse at Spanish City amusement park in 1961.

Darren Stevens and his son Martin enjoy an afternoon at Northumberland Park in 1990.

John Wright and Ann Watts outside St Peter's church on their wedding day in July 1967. The parents on each side of the happy couple are: Robert and Annie Fife Wright, and Doris and Jack Watts.

Other local titles published by The History Press

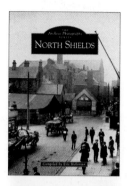

North Shields
ERIC HOLLERTON

With 200 photographs from the archives of the North Tyneside Libraries, this book on North Shields shows that this 'town where no town ought to be' has survived eight centuries with a multitude of stories. Looking along the riverside between Fish Quay and Smith's Dock, and the streets south of the road to Tynemouth, this book looks at local schools, leisure activities and transport, as well as North Shield's people.
07524 0730 9

Jarrow
PAUL PERRY

Jarrow was once a sparsely populated area which swelled to a population of 40,000 when industry boomed in the 1920s. Around ten years later, Jarrow faced decline. Using a fascinating collection of over 200 images, this book shows the rise, unexpected fall and further rise of Jarrow. Professional photographer Paul Perry also compiled *Jarrow Then & Now*, a pictorial history charting the changing face of the town and its skyline.
07524 3336 9

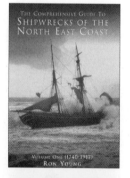

Shipwrecks of the North East Coast Volume one (1740-1917)
RON YOUNG

Sailors have long-since known the danger that both life at sea and the odd voyage into deep waters can bring. In this book, Ron Young, an experienced diver of many years, catalogues the demise of many ships along the north-east coast of England, from Whitby to Berwick-upon-Tweed, and tells the story of their last journey. He assesses the potential of the wrecks as dive-sites and remembers the bravery of lifeboat crews. This book is comprehensive and engrossing.
07524 1749 5

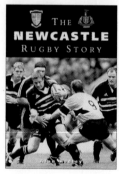

The Newcastle Rugby Story
ALAN HEDLEY

Rugby in the North East has a long illustrious history and intertwined with it is the story of the Newcastle club now known universally as The Falcons. This book remembers some of the clubs key moments, and passionate players. Written by Alan Hedley, a rugby journalist based in Newcastle for the last twenty-five years, this book is an essential read for any sport or rugby fan in the North East.
07524 2046 1

If you are interested in purchasing other books published by The History Press, or in case you have difficulty finding any of our books in your local bookshop, you can also place orders directly through our website
www.thehistorypress.co.uk